Hidden Harbours of Southwest Scotland

Published by
Imray Laurie Norie & Wilson Ltd
Wych House St Ives
Cambridgeshire PE27 5BT England
☎ +44 (0)1480 462114
Email ilnw@imray.com
www.imray.com
2015

© Text: Dag Pike 2015
© Photographs: Dag Pike 2015
© Aerial photographs: Getmapping plc 2015
© Plans: Imray Laurie Norie & Wilson Ltd 2015

All rights reserved. No part of this publication may be reproduced, transmitted or used in any form by any means – graphic, electronic or mechanical, including photocopying, recording, taping or information storage and retrieval systems or otherwise – without the prior permission of the Publishers.

Caution: To the extent permitted by law, the Publishers and Author do not accept liability for any loss and/or damage howsoever caused that may arise from reliance on this book nor for any error, omission or failure to update the information that they contain.

The plans in this book are not to be used for navigation.
They are designed to support the text and should at all times be used with navigational charts.

978 184623 702 7

British Library Cataloguing in Publication Data.
A catalogue record for this title is available from the British Library.

Printed in Singapore by Star Standard Industries Pte Ltd

Hidden Harbours
OF SOUTHWEST SCOTLAND
Dag Pike

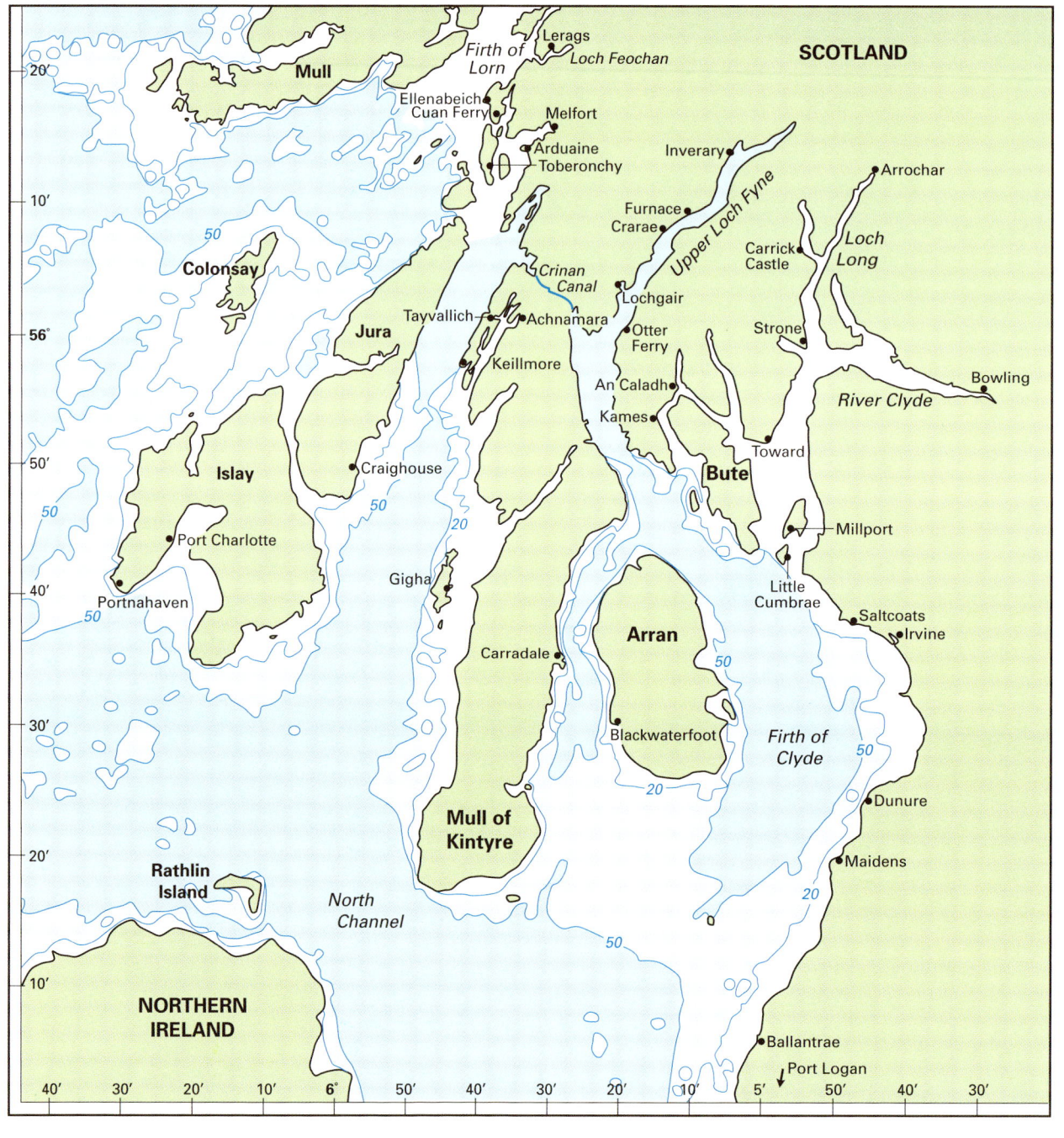

Contents

Introduction, 6

Port Logan, 10

Ballantrae, 12

Maidens, 14

Dunure, 16

Irvine, 18

Saltcoats, 20

Little Cumbrae, 22

Millport, 24

Bowling, 26

Arrochar, 28

Carrick Castle, 30

Strone, 32

Toward, 34

An Caladh, 36

Kames, 38

Otter Ferry, 40

Inverary, 42

Furnace, 44

Crarae, 46

Lochgair, 48

Carradale, 50

Blackwaterfoot, 52

Gigha, 54

Keillmore, 56

Tayvallich, 58

Achnamara, 60

Craighouse, 62

Port Charlotte and Bruinladdich, 64

Portnahaven, 66

Toberonchy, 68

Arduaine, 70

Melfort, 72

Cuan Ferry, 74

Ellenabeich and Easdale, 76

Lerags, 78

Introduction

The west coast of Scotland is one of the most beautiful cruising areas in the world. Towering mountains give way to long fingers of the sea that reach far inland creating a land and seascape that offers sheltered waters and stunning scenery. In the past this was a challenging area for transport by land and the whole economy was focused on the water, but today it is a tourist paradise accessible by both land and sea. To the west, the area between Oban to the north and the Mull of Galloway to the south is largely protected from Atlantic storms by the outlying islands but under the shelter of the land this area is a fascinating and rewarding cruising ground.

Coming in from seaward around the Mull of Kintyre you enter a sea full of history and wonderful scenery. The verdant green of the islands is in contrast to the calmer seas of the sheltered waters. Then further to the north the mountains close in and the land surrounds the long sea lochs that stretch for miles inland. Coming in from the south, from the Mull of Galloway the land is softer and lower-lying and it becomes increasingly industrialised as you approach the busy Clyde.

In the north, Oban is the gateway to many of the offshore islands and the rugged countryside to its south is dotted with remote communities. Throughout much of this area the tides can run strong between the islands. Fortunately, the notorious Corryvrecken whirlpool between the islands of Jura and Scarba is off the main cruising routes. These off-lying islands, such as Islay and Jura, have a character all of their own, with isolated communities and wild stretches of uninhabited moorland.

The Vikings saw the attraction of the area, with parts of it resembling their native fjords, and they used the Firth of Clyde as the gateway to explore much of Scotland. The existence of old castles along many of the shores is an indication of the turmoil of the past but today the castles are much more likely to be the magnificent houses of the aristocrats and rich industrialists who established estates in the region. There is history in every mile you sail and in every step you take amongst the dramatic scenery of this region.

When I first sailed in this area it was very basic sailing indeed and rather than entering a marina at night you would find a quiet anchorage and be the only yacht in sight. You had to be truly self-sufficient and to fill up with fresh water you might take the tender ashore and fill up from a local burn. For company you might find wildlife, such as seals, gathering around your boat and the peace and quiet were a joy to experience. Today you can still find these remote spots but you have to look much harder to find them and the character of the cruising grounds has changed quite dramatically, particularly in those areas that are easy to reach from main cities.

The vistas stretch forever on Scotland's west coast

Now there are enough marinas to undertake marina cruising where you can walk ashore every night from your marina berth and have all the facilities of home on your doorstep. Even the smaller harbours in some of the more remote areas provide pontoons for visitors, whilst many of the quiet and remote anchorages are now filled with permanent moorings making it harder to find that quiet anchorage of the past.

This has not changed the stunning scenery. Mountains provide a dramatic backdrop to the lochs and, despite considerable development in the form of military installations and other facilities around the Firth of Clyde, the effect on the beauty of the landscape is minimal. In fact, you may only become aware of these developments if your movements are restricted by large ships or submarines.

Wartime demands brought new activities to these wild and remote waters. The deep and sheltered waters of the lochs meant that they could play host to ocean-going ships and in wartime they were used for convoy assembly as well as bases for naval ships. There is an abandoned torpedo base at the head of Loch Long and training bases for a variety of purposes were established along the shores of many of the lochs. Oban to the north and Loch Ryan in the south were bases for many of the North Atlantic operations during World War II. Later, during the Cold War, the United States based some of their nuclear submarines in Holy Loch.

Today the British Trident submarines have their base at Faslane on Gare Loch and NATO has a fuel depot on Loch Long, which brings tankers into the area. Although many of the wartime facilities have now found a civilian use as boatyards and marinas, the military presence is still significant.

In much of the southern region covered in this book the land is softer and more rounded than in the wilder country further north but in the past it was largely cut off from the outside world, relying on subsistence farming and fishing to support the isolated communities. There was little in the way of natural resources and the main exports to nearby cities such as Glasgow were timber from the forests, quarried stone, dried fish and live cattle. Transport was almost always by sea, with the penetrating lochs providing a sheltered route to Glasgow and the open sea. This trade led to the development of a specialised vessel capable of navigating the waters under sail but with a flat bottom that enabled it to be beached for the unloading of cargo at low water. As well as exporting the aforementioned goods, these small cargo ships would bring in coal and manufactured goods for the isolated local communities.

In the mid 1800s, as sail gave way to steam, these small sailing ships were replaced by a unique style of cargo boat, the Clyde Puffer. The boats were originally designed to operate on the newly constructed Clyde and Forth Canal and because they were operating in fresh water they did not have to condense the steam from the engine. Instead this was

Fishing is still important but the catches have changed

The channels and islands of the west coast make a magnificent cruising area

exhausted through the funnel in 'puffs', hence the name. They proved to be the ideal cargo boat for serving the remote communities along the shores of the lochs. For this work in salt water the engines were fitted with condensers so that the fresh water could be extracted and reused in the boilers. This meant there were no more puffs from the funnel but the name remained and is immortalised in Neil Munro's famous book *Para Handy*.

The Clyde Puffer was the key to the opening up of the lochs and offshore islands to the outside world, providing the essential transport link for the loch-side communities. The opening of the Crinan Canal across the top end of the Kintyre Peninsula gave these small ships access to the Western Isles and up to Oban without them having to negotiate the exposed and often dangerous seas off the Mull of Kintyre. Larger versions of the Puffer were built to cope with these outside waters up to the maximum size that could be accommodated by the canal locks.

The world's first steam passenger ship, the *Comet*, was built in Glasgow to provide a passenger service out of Glasgow to some of the nearby coastal towns on the islands and lochs of the Clyde estuary. From this humble beginning there developed a maze of passenger routes out of Glasgow, forming an escape route for the workers of the shipyards and coal mines in the area. This led to a rapid growth in passenger services to the western waters. As with the Clyde Puffer, a whole new breed of ship was spawned to meet the demands of these busy passenger routes. Fast steamers were brought into service, carrying passengers to resorts such as Dunoon and Rothesay, which became the fashionable places to escape the industrial smog of the cities and began to open the Western Isles and lochs to the outside world. Piers were built at many of the smaller communities to allow the passenger ships to come alongside and the waters were criss-crossed with passenger routes. The ships were an advanced form of paddle steamer with speeds of up to 20 knots and helped to put the Clyde on the map as the world's primary shipbuilding centre.

Today these paddle steamer services have been replaced by the vastly improved roads that wind around the edges of the lochs and islands and by the ubiquitous CalMac steamers that provide the essential links to many destinations, including the islands. MacBrayne operate the CalMac ferries as well as many of the bus routes and form an essential transport link for both the local communities and the tourists that visit the area. Now government owned, MacBrayne is as much part of highland scenery as are the mountains and lochs. In the past there were also many ferries that bridged the entrances to the long lochs snaking inland. They were operated to help shorten the distances for land travel and some do remain but the CalMac steamers now principally connect the islands such as Islay, Bute, Arran and Jura to the mainland. Operating from bases at Oban and West Loch Tarbet and with some links further south, these steamers, transporting cars, trucks and passengers, are an essential part of the landscape of western Scotland.

The development of industry has been largely confined to the south of the region, with the focus around the Clyde and extending along to harbours to its south. The shipbuilding trade has been responsible for opening up many of these harbours to the south of the Clyde; places like Troon and Ayr had shipyards that focussed on smaller ships, whilst

The MacBrayne steamers are the lifeline of the islands

many of the smaller harbours along this coast were constructed to support the fishing fleets that were exploiting the fishing grounds offshore. These were busy waters playing host to cargo, passenger and fishing vessels and their easy access to the open Atlantic Ocean encouraged the expanding transatlantic trade.

The character of this whole region is changing, not just in terms of the military and commercial presence but also with regard to tourism in the area. In the past people came to this area because it was wild and remote and the facilities were few and far between. Today you can still get that sense of wilderness but you will also see changes, with improved roads and ever increasing facilities such as hotels and restaurants. The improved infrastructure has opened the area up to greatly increased tourism, which has obviously helped the local economy but for the sailor has taken away some of the thrill of sailing into quiet and remote areas. However, these can still be found in some of the sea lochs south of Oban, where the only disturbance during a night at anchor is likely to come from the wildlife rather than from human interference. Likewise, out on the islands, it is still a very different way of life and it is intriguing on Islay to find that most of the hidden harbours on the island have been developed to serve the many distilleries that line the shores.

There are many so-called harbours in the region that are simply piers or slipways built to serve the ferry trade and which offer little in the way of history and interest. There are many more, tucked away, that have been built to serve local needs, perhaps to provide shelter for Clyde Puffers or for local fishing boats. With such a wide selection of harbours to choose from it has been a challenge to pick between them but in this book the emphasis, as far as possible, has been on the hidden harbours, the ones off the beaten track and those that have history and a story to tell.

Dramatic weather on the west coast

Port Logan

History and comments

Located just a short hop north of the Mull of Galloway, Port Logan dates back to the 17th century when it was called Port Nessock. The original pier here was built by the local laird who also developed the village as a small fishing port. 130 years later a descendent of this laird, Colonel Andrew McDougall, promoted the idea of expanding the harbour and called in engineer John Rennie. Work eventually got underway in 1818 and two years later the harbour, as you see it today, was completed.

The original plans envisaged a breakwater enclosing the whole bay but only the section to the south of the bay was included in the final construction. This provides a remarkably sheltered harbour even in strong winds, helped considerably by the ridge of half tide rocks that extends out from the end of the breakwater. The ridge provides good shelter for the small space inside but it presents a considerable hazard when entering the harbour.

A key feature of the new harbour construction was a causeway running across the front of the houses in the village. The layout of these houses has been reversed, with the bedrooms downstairs and living spaces upstairs, so as to maintain the view over the causeway. The harbour was originally intended as a landing point for the cattle trade from

Ireland but it reverted to its original use as a fishing port with the construction of a fish pond to the north of the harbour to store fresh fish.

The most remarkable feature of the harbour is the grand stone lighthouse on the pier head, originally designed to house a fire to guide the boats home. The pier is solidly constructed from local stone and sits for the most part atop a natural ridge of rocks, which runs out from the shore.

A lifeboat station was established here in 1866 but closed down in 1932. The lifeboat house remains and is now the village hall, whilst the

Even in winter, Port Logan is a safe harbour

slipway down which the lifeboat was launched now serves as a boat launch.

Access by road
From the main road to Stranraer take the B7084 and then the A718 before turning right onto the road signposted to Port Logan.

Parking
On land around the harbour.

Water access
Easy access from seaward with the pier head lighthouse as a guide but give the pier end a wide berth, about the same length as the pier, away from the pier head. Space inside is very limited and mainly occupied by local boats.

Facilities
The Port Logan Inn is temporarily closed and there is no date for reopening.

Further information
None available.

Postcode
DG9 9QU

The old stone lighthouse on the pierhead, where fires would be lit to guide the boats home

Far left Granite mooring posts are a legacy from the past

Ballantrae

History and comments

Located close to the main shipping routes to and from the Clyde, Ballantrae has a long maritime history of shipwrecks and smuggling. This colourful past is remembered at the village's summer Smuggler's Festival.

Fishing was Ballantrae's main occupation day to day, with boats working off the beach and using the entrance to the River Stinchar south of the town as a small harbour, accessible when the weather was favourable.

The river entrance has moved around considerably over the years and its unreliability as a natural harbour led to the construction of an artificial one in 1847 at a cost of £6,000. The pier was constructed using red sandstone imported from Arran and allowed larger fishing boats to safely operate from Ballantrae, although the harbour dried out at low water. It is reported that the steamer from Stranraer to Glasgow made occasional calls at the harbour and small coastal vessels, probably Clyde Puffers, called with cargoes of coal and agricultural products.

When the lucrative cod fishery offshore went into decline the vessels in the harbour followed suit. The harbour is now used during the summer months by a small number of fishing and angling boats, with the professionals mainly engaged in potting. The harbour was gifted to the Ballantrae Community Council in the 1990s and whilst visiting yachts can

The wooden post used to check the launching of the lifeboat

Right *The remains of the stone boathouse and the tower on the hill, which helps to locate the harbour from seaward*

The pier built from red sandstone

use it, access to much of the quay wall is obstructed by mooring lines.

The lifeboat station established at Ballantrae in the 1860s was disbanded in 1917 but the lifeboat house on the shore side of the harbour remains and is used as a store. The slipway down which the lifeboat was launched is now a launching ramp for boats but the strong wooden post at the top of the slip, originally used to hold the lifeboat, is still standing.

The remains of a stone boathouse built in the 19th century can still be seen along the shore and it appears to be in the process of being restored. It is a tribute to the sturdy construction of this harbour that it still remains in good shape after 160 years of battering by the westerly gales.

Access by road

From the A77, the main road through the town, take Shore Road to the beach and turn right towards the harbour.

Parking

In the street or close by the harbour.

Water access

A tower on the hull above the harbour provides a guide to the entrance. Pass close to the end of the pier before turning sharply to avoid a rocky ridge running out from the shore. The harbour dries completely at low water and has mooring ropes in the summer months.

Facilities

Typical of a small town.

Further information

Ballantrae Community Council
mlm@doctors.org.uk

Postcode

KA26 0NX

Maidens

The rocks and breakwater combine to provide shelter to the harbour

History and comments

Like most of the smaller harbours along this Ayrshire coastline, Maidens started life as a fishing harbour. Taking advantage of the rocks lying off the shore, the harbour provided shelter from the onshore winds with a small pier jutting out from the shore. The approach channel meandered through a gap in the rocks and the prolific fishing grounds in the seas off this coastline provided a good living for the fishermen.

When trade in the harbour grew, the present harbour was built to provide better shelter for the local shipyard and for use by the ships that brought in supplies of coal for the local gasworks. Maidens Harbour was built by the Marquis of Ailsa in the mid-19th century and when first constructed it

consisted of a stone pier running out from the small headland that forms the focus of the harbour. It is thought that a smaller stone pier once formed a minor harbour outside the line of the present pier, this would have been the original fishing harbour.

The present harbour has been extended out to the north with a concrete pier linking the various groups of rocks that previously formed a natural breakwater protecting the entrance channel.

The local shipyard established by the Marquis was named the Culzean Steam Launch and Yacht Works. It later moved to Troon to become the famous Ailsa Shipyard. The yard at Maidens built over 60 yachts, including the famous line of Shamrock yachts that challenged for the early America's Cup. After World War II, fishing declined and activity in Maidens Harbour greatly decreased. The majority of cargo was now brought in and out by road.

In 1953 the remaining local fishermen joined with the council to fund substantial improvements to the harbour, which was handed over to the local authority by the Culzean Estate during this same period.

In 1988 it was sold to the Maidens Harbour Trust for £100 with the purpose of preserving the harbour and preventing large-scale marina development on the site. Now, with pontoons for both visitors and the local fishing fleet and dredging to maintain the entrance channel, Maidens is a viable small port that supports the local community.

Access by road
From the A719 make a sharp turn to the west by the Turnbury Apartments and follow Harbour Road directly to the harbour.

Parking
Limited parking on the road and in the harbour.

Water access
Although surrounded by rocks, the entrance to Maidens is available in most weathers. Painted wooden poles mark the channel. There is a sharp turn to starboard as the harbour channel opens up. The breakwater to the east is largely covered at high water.

Facilities
The facilities of a small town, plus the major golf course of Turnbury and its facilities just two miles to the south.

Further information
www.maidensharbour.co.uk
Harbourmaster ☎ 07854 118277

Postcode
KA26 9NR

A fishing boat weather vane

The modern finger jetties make a good mooring for boats

Dunure

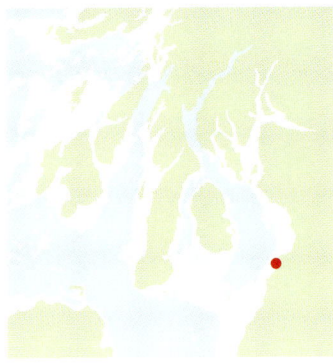

History and comments

Dunure is a very interesting harbour created from a rocky beach. It was constructed in 1811, to a design by Thomas Kennedy, at a cost of £50,000, which was a lot of money in those days. It was built for the export of coal from a local coalmine but when this trade ceased it became a harbour for fishing boats. Fishing boats, and more recently angling boats, remain its primary users to this day.

In the original designs for the harbour there was an option for a more expensive harbour, which would have had an outer breaker protecting the entrance from the prevailing southwesterly winds. The cheaper version was built and does have severe tidal restrictions, being only accessible from about half tide onwards. With onshore winds the entrance has heavy breaking seas, which can make it a dangerous place for those unfamiliar with it.

The harbour basin itself was blasted out of the solid rock on the shore and given a layer of puddled clay on its bottom for the boats to sit on when the tide ebbed. The main dock area is on the starboard side coming in from the entrance channel and is marked by a stubby round tower where a bonfire lighthouse would be lit to help boats negotiate the entrance at night.

Fishing boats used the harbour as a base for over 100 years but in the 1960s, as the size of fishing boats grew, the harbour was no longer viable for them. They moved out allowing leisure fishing boats and yachts to take over and today the harbour is used almost entirely by leisure craft. These moor in the basin but there is also scope for trailer launching from a slipway at the head of the main entrance channel.

The weather beaten watch tower at the entrance

The harbour is owned by the Baron of Dunure and is currently leased to a local harbour association which is active both in the operation of the harbour and the planning of restoration work and developments to encourage visiting yachts. To the south of the harbour are the towering remains of Dunure Castle, which was, at one time, home to the Kennedy family who built the harbour.

Access by road
The main coast road, the A719 passes close alongside the harbour and a turning to the south of the harbour gives direct access.

Parking
There is some parking on the quay and road parking in the village.

Water access
The entrance channel is between banks of rocks, with the light tower giving an indication of the run of the channel. The line of the north pier also shows the line of the entrance channel. Turn immediately to starboard on passing the tower to enter the basin. Finding a berth could be a challenge, although there are plans to make Dunure more accessible for visiting yachts.

Facilities
The Dunure Inn is on the quay and has a good reputation for food. A coffee house/café is close by and there is a shop in the village.

Further information
Dunure Harbour Committee Association Ltd
jeanmcginn@tiscali.co.uk

Postcode
KA7 4LN

The bar across the entrance can be dangerous in onshore winds

The square harbour basin was cut out of solid rock

Irvine

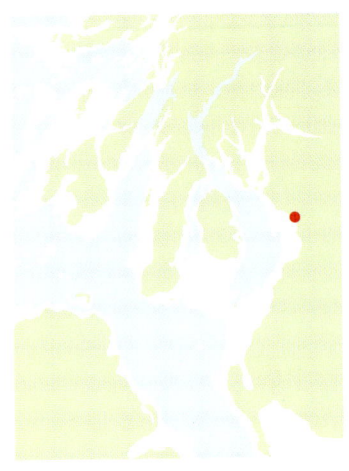

History and comments

Irvine has a long maritime history, with records dating back to the 10th century. At one time it was a major port serving the whole of Ayrshire and the Glasgow area. It was used as a port for shipping out coal from nearby mines, most of it destined for Ireland and had its own shipyards, one of which remained active up until World War II. However, the depth limitations of its entrance channel and the deepening of the channel into the Clyde eventually led to its demise as a harbour.

Up until fairly recently Irvine was the location of a major chemical industry and the ICI Nobel explosives facility was located on the northern shore. The factory was closed down in 1990 but the quay and channel used by the coastal ships which serviced it both remain. Much of the more remote north bank was taken over by NPL Estates when the factory closed and they redeveloped the area with the Big Idea, an impressive exhibition and social arena. This closed in 2003 due to low visitor numbers but it is hoped that it will reopen as part of a golfing complex. The Big Idea centre is connected to the south shore and the town by a sliding

footbridge that now remains almost permanently open to let boats past.

Today Irvine looks a little sad and is a harbour in transition. The Scottish Maritime Museum has been established here and uses the old shipyard slipway area for some of its exhibits. Pontoons for visiting yachts have been built on the south shore of the harbour and some of the museum exhibits, such as the Clyde Puffers, lie here as well.

The entrance channel is wide open to the west, although the fetch is limited by the islands offshore. There is adequate water for entry at most states of

There is still much work to be done to make Irvine attractive to visiting yachts

tide and the channel is focussed by submerged stone breakwaters. The Pilots' Tower, which once had tidal signals displayed on its roof, makes a useful entry landmark; it is a four-storey, square, white tower on the south side of the entrance. The area around the tower has been landscaped as part of the ongoing regeneration scheme that could eventually make Irvine an attractive harbour for visitors.

Access by road

The A78 bypasses the town but follow the signs to the centre and then continue heading west and following the signs to the Magnum leisure centre, close by the harbour. Two tall factory chimneys can provide a useful guide.

Parking

Roadside parking and a car park on the south side of the harbour entrance.

Water access

A beacon marks the harbour entrance and the Pilots' Tower provides a good guide from offshore. It is reported that there are depths of approximately 1 metre in the channel at low water but there can be heavy breaking seas with onshore winds. Inside, the channel is marked by wooden poles and the footbridge is normally kept open.

The pontoons are the main visitor moorings

Facilities

All the facilities expected of a town. The Ship Inn and other facilities on the quay, close by the pontoons.

Further information

The Irvine Harbour Co. www.irvineharbour.com
Harbourmaster ☏ 0141 2427900

Postcode

KA12 8PZ

The exposed entrance channels are marked by posts

Saltcoats

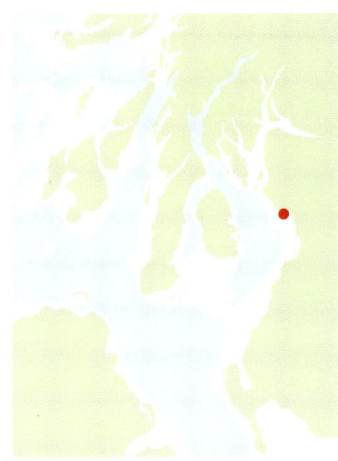

History and comments

The harbour at Saltcoats was built in 1686 for the export of coal from the nearby Stevenston coalfields. It is reported that a canal was built along the two-mile route from the coalfields to the harbour to facilitate the transport of the coal; some traces of this canal can still be seen today. The canal did not quite reach the harbour and the final part of the journey had to be made by cart, which seems a strange arrangement.

Incorporated into the harbour on the shore side, where the supermarket now stands, were saltpans: large containers filled with seawater and sat above a coal fire for the production of salt via evaporation. The coal was readily available via the canal, which could explain why it did not quite reach the harbour. The town got its name from these saltpans and they continued operating right up until 1890.

When the harbour was first built it had a simple L-shaped pier that extended out from the shore but in 1800 an outer pier was added to give more shelter to the inner section and provide additional space. A rather grand round tower with a light was added on the end of the outer pier to guide shipping to the harbour. At this time Saltcoats was a busy harbour, suited to the size of the ships in use at that time for the trade between Saltcoats and Ireland.

In 1914 the harbour was purchased by the town and renovated, as described by a plaque on the outer pier head. Shipbuilding was carried out in the harbour and there was also a strong fishing fleet based there.

Today the coalfields have closed, the saltpans have gone and competition from the nearby port of Ardrossan, with its deeper water and better facilities, has greatly reduced the activity in the harbour. The harbour is now used for the most part by local boats and appears to have made little attempt to attract visiting yachts.

There is a rather sad, run-down look about the harbour and the empty house on the quay that once served as the custom house and harbour office adds to the sense of abandonment. The harbour remains intact but the addition of a supermarket and rather bland housing along the waterfront has destroyed much of the atmosphere.

The outer basin at Saltcoats can be quite exposed

Access by road
From the main A78 take the A738 into town and then the B 714 to the harbour area.

Parking
There is a pay and display car park on the harbour front next to the supermarket car park.

Water access
Pick out the tower on the end of the outer breakwater as a guide in but give the pier head a good clearance to avoid the rocks that extend out from its end. Then keep close to the inner pier to avoid the rocks on the north side of the harbour. The harbour dries at low water.

Facilities
All the facilities of a small town.

Further information
☏ 01294 225200

Postcode
KA21 5EP

The history of the harbour is remembered in a bronze plaque

Rocks extend out from the pierhead, which is marked by its distinctive tower

Little Cumbrae

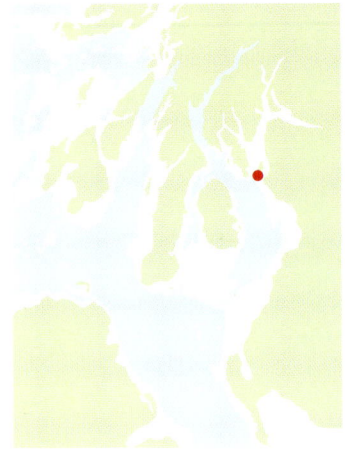

History and comments

This strategically placed island guards the entrance to the Clyde Estuary, yet, apart from a small castle on its eastward side, it is surprisingly unfortified. The castle was built in the 16th century on a small island just off the east side of Little Cumbrae. It is cut off by the tide at high water and is believed to have been built to stop poaching on the island.

There were proposals to build a small harbour on the island in the past but the island residents were against the idea, wanting to maintain their isolation. The current stone pier just inshore from the castle is, therefore, a relatively recent addition. The large house close to the castle was built at the turn of the 20th century, the same period in which the current harbour was built.

The strategic location of Little or 'Wee' Cumbrae made it the chosen site for one of the earliest lighthouses in Scotland. It was built on the highest point of the island, with the light coming from a coal fire on top of the tower. Later, towards the end of the 18th century, a new lighthouse was built on the southwest corner of the island, closer to sea level. This was powered by oil lamps and, later, by electricity. The current modern light positioned close by is solar powered and unmanned but the slipway and steps that were used to bring stores to the manned lighthouse still exist, although they are reported as breaking up.

This little gem of an island was last sold in 2009. Now privately owned, with the main house used as a yoga centre, the island is reportedly up for sale once more and at the time of writing its future looks uncertain. There have been various plans to exploit the island for commercial purposes, one of which included the development of a 40 berth marina, plus the usual holiday homes that go with such a project.

The stone pier that serves as the main access to the island is rare in that it is accessible at all states of tide. It has a berth alongside on the small T-head. The structure is solidly built with timber facing and looks to be in good repair. It is reported that the

public can access the island but there is no regular boat service and the only residents are two caretakers for the house.

Access by road
No road access.

Parking
No parking.

Water access
The jetty is accessible at all states of tide for shallow draft boats but approach from the north and use the west face of the jetty as a line for the entry channel.

Facilities
None

Further information
None

Postcode
None

The lighthouse and its solar panels

HIDDEN HARBOURS OF SOUTHWEST SCOTLAND   23

Above The castle dominates the entrance to the sheltered harbour

The abandoned pier built to serve the lighthouse

Millport

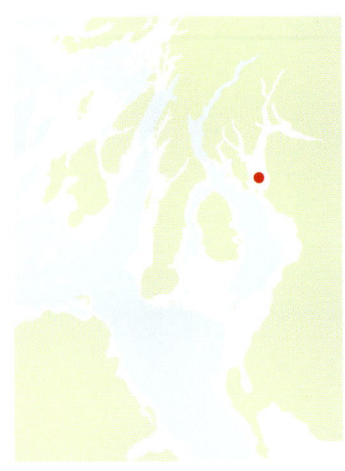

The main pier at Millport, developed to cope with the tourist trade

History and comments

Millport is the main town on the island of Great Cumbrae and the establishment of the harbour here owes much to the island's strategic location at the entrance to the Clyde and to the presence of the various ports and harbours further north. In the 1600s Millport was the base for a small revenue cutter that patrolled the estuary waters and the original harbour, tucked inside a rocky outcrop extending into the bay and further protected by the offshore islands, dates from this time.

The harbour was enlarged in the 18th century when a larger and faster revenue cutter was introduced and much of the town was developed at this time to provide accommodation for the crew. The harbour also became busy with the export of stone from a nearby quarry; this stone was the favoured material for the construction of harbour walls and was also used in the construction of the Caledonian Canal.

In 1833 a company was formed to further develop the harbour and the pier was extended to

allow access for landing passengers from the Clyde steamers at all states of tide. The harbour was also a busy fishing port, with upwards of 40 boats operating from it.

By 1860 Millport was a popular tourist destination and the pier was extended yet further, to its present size. The influx of tourists led to Millport becoming more of a holiday resort than a commercial port.

Today Millport harbour is home to a small number of local fishing and leisure boats and the pier is principally a landing point for visitors from ships in the bay. The establishment of the ferry service from Largs to the island, which lands further north, on the east shore of Cumbrae, has taken away much of the traffic into Millport but it remains a visiting place for yachts and free moorings can be found in the bay to the east of the harbour. Its closeness to the mainland means that Millport is easily accessible for day trips, as such, the town becomes busy in the summer months.

There are adequate facilities for visitors onshore. The pier is deteriorating and only smaller vessels are allowed alongside these days. The Cathedral of the Isles, located just inland from the harbour, is well worth a visit.

Access by road
Take the ferry from Largs to the island and then follow the signposted road south to Millport.

Parking
Parking on the street and at the quay.

Water access
Access to the moorings is straightforward but to reach the harbour you must negotiate the channels between the off-lying rocks/islands.

Facilities
All the facilities of a small town, including bike hire, golf and pubs.

Further information
Isle of Cumbrae Tourist Association
www.millport.org

Postcode
KA28 0AS

The entrance on the right is the original harbour

History is seen in the original granite bollards

Bowling

History and comments

The area around Bowling has a long history dating back over 5000 years and it has been occupied by both the Romans and the Vikings. In more recent history, Bowling was the chosen entrance to the Forth and Clyde Canal which, when it was built in 1790, had its own entrance directly into the River Clyde. The Bowling Basin lies outside the canal area and when it was constructed in 1846, it was developed via a river wall extending from the old canal lock to enclose quite a section of the bank of the Clyde. It included a second lock entrance to the canal with direct access from the tidal basin; this is the canal entrance that is in use today.

Today the eastern section of the river wall that enclosed the basin lies in ruin and is partly covered at high tide but the entrance gap remains as the access point to the canal lock.

Like so much of the River Clyde, the Bowling Basin was principally used for shipbuilding and the main yard located there was Scott and Sons. This shipyard began life in 1800, using the dry dock, which was located inside the canal basin, shortly after the canal was opened. However, in 1846 when the canal basin was being enlarged, the dry dock was closed and the shipyard was moved to the western

end of the Bowling Basin from where it continued to operate until 1979. Scott and Sons were responsible for building 40 of the Clyde Puffers; around 10% of the total fleet. They were also well known for building tugs, coastal ships and fishing boats. The basin was used to moor up ships waiting to enter the shipyard and later as a winter lay-up location for leisure craft.

With the restoration of the canal, the basin's main function became that of providing access to the lock. Accordingly, action was taken to remove many of

Wrecks still litter the old Bowling Basin

the ship remains that had littered the basin since it became a dumping ground for redundant ships. A few of these wrecks remain on the northern side.

The basin dries out completely at low water and offers a few drying moorings. It is dominated by the railway bridge and huge white custom house, and is a busy area, which has been developed for leisure use. The whole of the canal above the lock entrance is full of moored leisure craft and there are plans for further development and a tidy up of the area. If the plans go ahead, it seems likely that the basin will become a nature reserve.

Access by road
From the A82 main road, take the A814 at the first roundabout after the Erskine bridge junction. The basin can be seen on the right and a small sign indicates a right turn over the railway bridge into the canal basin.

Parking
It is not signposted but take a sharp right turn up a narrow lane between high walls and the railway, then pass under the railway bridge after which the parking area for the canal basin will be revealed.

Water access
From the main river channel take a port turn between the two wooden posts that mark the entrance to the channel leading to the canal lock entrance.

Facilities
The Bay Inn in Bowling and some shops and further facilities in Old Kirkpatrick to the east. Water and toilets are in the canal basin surroundings.

Further information
Harbour office ☎ 01389 877969

Postcode
G60 5AQ

The lock entrance to the Forth and Clyde Canal from the basin

The basin looks a welcoming sight at high water but dries at low water

Arrochar

The decaying remains of the steamer pier at Arrochar

History and comments

Arrochar lies at the head of Loch Long, occupying a strategic location from a land point of view. The Vikings are reported to have landed here in the 13th century. Coming in from the sea, Arrochar is the final destination after the long journey up the loch and was opened up when the Clyde steamers made the village a port of call. This led to the development of hotels in the village and the expansion of the tourist trade.

Today the village still attracts visitors but the vast majority come by road as the town lies close to the main road into the Highlands and is also served by rail. This is an attractive spot for yachts, however, its

distance from the waters to the south means that few yachts make the long journey up the loch and consequently there are limited facilities for yachts in the area.

The two steamer piers have fallen into disrepair and only their rusting remains can still be seen. Much of the decline in the sea-going trade in the area can be ascribed to the arrival of the railway in the village, which makes it one of the few harbours in the highlands connected by rail and provides much easier access to Glasgow than by sea.

Today Arrochar is a tranquil spot with a stunning mountain backdrop well worth a visit by water. There are some moorings in the bay but these appear to be for local use and there are no dedicated visitors' moorings. Landing is possible at a slipway at the base of the remains of the upper pier.

Across the water are the remains of the Arrochar torpedo testing facility that was erected in 1912 and only decommissioned in 1986. The site included a pier with buildings on it. The torpedoes were fired from tubes installed beneath the pier and tracked as they went down the long straight loch. The buildings above the pier housed the torpedoes which could be lowered directly down into the firing tubes and a boat stood by to recover the torpedoes for analysis after the run. The pier was in the process of being dismantled when it caught fire and is currently in a very sad state, with no known plans for its future.

Access by road
Arrochar lies at the junction of the A83, the main route into the west, and the A814, with the village lying along both roads.

Parking
Free on street parking can be busy in summer.

Water access
Straight up Loch Long with no dangers but the water shallows approaching the head of the loch.

The landing steps and slipway are convenient for the pub

Facilities
Hotels, pubs, restaurants and a shop.

Further information
Tourist Information Centre in Tarbet
www.arrochar.org.uk
☎ 01301 702260

Postcode
G83 7AB

Carrick Castle

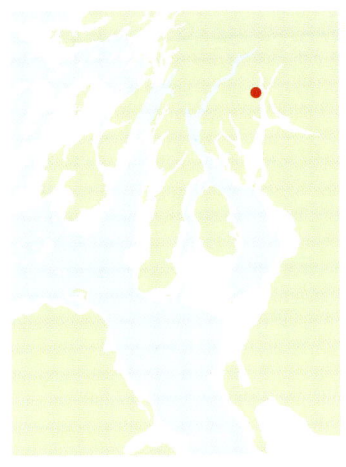

History and comments

The castle at Carrick Castle is a prime example of the fortifications that were built around the sea lochs in the 14th century, during the turbulent times of clan fighting in this region. This was one of the homes of the Campbell clan and it lies in a striking location upon a rocky spit that juts out into Loch Goil, creating not only a dramatic addition to the landscape but also making a fine navigation mark. It is thought that there were previous castles built upon this spot, although little evidence remains.

For years the current castle stood abandoned and falling into decay but today a new owner has started its long restoration. Evidence of this can be seen in

The mooring area at Carrick with one of the MOD range marks

the new roof, complete with Velux windows, which has made the building weather tight. It is thought that there is work going on inside to restore the interior into a private dwelling.

Under the new ownership the castle and the peninsula on which it stands is private and fenced off. This prevents any access to the pier, which is a more recent addition and extends out into the loch from the castle. The pier looks to be a modern construction and is thought to have been built by the Ministry of Defence for use by the MOD boats that patrolled the sound range located further up the loch, at Lochgoilhead. Today the connection between the pier head and the land has been removed but what looks like the original stone pier that served the castle and the pier head structure remain.

For visiting boats there is a good mooring area located just inside the bight formed by the castle outcrop and the next headland. This is managed by the Castle Carrick Boat Club, which has permits for 50 moorings in the area. Most are occupied by local boats but there are blue visitors' mooring buoys available on payment of a fee. These moorings occupy most of the available space so anchoring is not viable here but could be possible in the more exposed area to the south of the castle.

Landing by tender is on the beach. The hotel on the waterfront that might previously have provided a focus for a visit has been converted into apartments but even these are currently closed, although whether this is temporary or permanent is not known.

Access by road
Take the single-track road south from Lochgoilhead.

Parking
In the hotel/apartment area or on the road.

The castle and the remains of the pier at Carrick Castle

Water access
Enter Loch Goil from Loch Long, Carrick Castle is seen to port. There may be temporary restrictions on access if trials are taking place at the MOD range.

Facilities
None except a picnic area by the castle.

Further information
Carrick Castle Boat Club ☏ 01301 703098
www.carrick-castle-boat-club.co.uk

Postcode
PA24 8AF

Strone

History and comments

Strone is more of a headland than a harbour and it lies at the strategic junction of Holy Loch and Loch Long, with the narrowing Clyde estuary passing its door. The village stretches right around the headland; the steep hills behind have prevented expansion inland, apart from the prominent house close to the point. The 'harbour' at Strone is in the form of three piers, two of which were built for the passenger steamers from Glasgow.

Strone's proximity to Glasgow enabled the village became established as a significant visitor destination for the citizens of Glasgow. Many established summer houses along the shore and commuter ferry services ran to and from Glasgow.

Today, Strone is a mixture of residential properties and summer homes. There is good road access so the three piers that were established to serve the steamers are now either derelict or used more for longer-term mooring. On the more sheltered Holy Loch side, close to where the US nuclear submarines were based, there is a large collection of moorings for yachts. The piers on this side also serve as a landing point, particularly Strone Pier, which gives direct access to the Strone Inn just across the road.

The two piers on the northern shore of Holy Loch, Strone and Kilmun have their landward section built of stone. These were later extended with a timber T-head, like so many of the Scottish steamer piers. Kilmun Pier was originally used for loading timber from the nearby forests into ships, today it is used by Western Ferries as a place to berth their Dunoon to Gourock ferries when they are not in use and is a gated pier with no public access. Strone Pier looks more or less abandoned apart from

Holy Loch with Kilmun Pier on the left

Blairmore Pier with the old ticket office, now a private home

The seemingly abandoned main pier at Strone

the access it provides to the Strone Inn. A ferry service used to run across from Holy Loch to Sandbanks on the south side but this ceased operation in 1970 when road access improved. The piers came back into use as a landing point when the US Navy brought their nuclear submarines into Holy Loch but these have long since departed and peace has returned to the area.

Around the corner on the Loch Long side there is the restored Blairmore Pier with its beautiful Victorian ticket office now converted into a private house. This is one of the best kept piers of the many steamer piers in the region and it is occasionally visited by the one remaining paddle steamer, *Waverley*.

Access by road
Strone lies on the A880 road that runs around the headland on the north side of Holy Loch with the road ending on the south side of Loch Long.

Parking
Free roadside parking.

Water access
Straight into Holy Loch with no obstructions except for rocks off the headland, which are marked by a buoy.

Facilities
The Strone Inn and a village store/Post Office at Blairmore, by the pier.

Further information
Strone Inn, previously know as the Argyll Hotel, provides moorings for customers.
www.stroneinn.co.uk
☏ 01369 840243

Postcode
PA23 8TA

Toward

History and comments

Toward Point is a significant headland on the Clyde Estuary, marked by a large white lighthouse that helps guide ships into port. There is a small landing slipway by the lighthouse itself but along the coast to the west is Toward harbour which is dominated by the magnificent Toward Castle, built in 1820 by the then Lord Provost of Glasgow as his country seat. Since then the castle has passed through several owners and is currently under the ownership of Argyll and Bute council who are trying to sell it or find alternative uses for it.

In the grounds of the 'modern' castle are the ruins of an earlier castle built in the 15th century. The small harbour on the foreshore below the main harbour was originally built to bring in stone for the building of the castle and was no doubt also used for supplies for the castle and the local village as well as the shipping out of agricultural produce to the mainland, just a short distance away.

The breakwater is built from stone, in an L-shape with the usual granite bollards, and it offers protection when the winds are blowing up the Firth of Clyde.

During the war the castle was a base for Combined Operations and just around the corner there are the remains of a larger harbour that was constructed during the war and used for training the crews of landing craft. Part of this 'new' harbour is the base for a fish farm.

The Towards Sailing Club clubhouse now dominates the old harbour. It is a cheap-looking modern building, unsympathetic to the magnificent surroundings. Painted in a strident blue and white, the club is the base for an active sailing club but it is out of character with the castle entrance building

The unsympathetic Toward Sailing Club clubhouse contrasts with the castle entrance behind

HIDDEN HARBOURS OF SOUTHWEST SCOTLAND 35

Access by road
Take the long winding coast road, the A815 south from Dunoon. This forks at its southern end with the left arm going to the lighthouse and the right one first to the village and then on to the castle and sailing club.

Parking
Alongside the harbour and the sailing club.

Water access
The sailing club acts as a guide coming in from seaward and the breakwater is located on the right of the clubhouse. The harbour dries at low water.

Facilities
A village store in Toward, about half a mile away, and the facilities at the sailing club when open.

Further information
Sailing Club mikegis@hotmail.co.uk
☏ 01369 706971
www.towardsc.org.uk

Postcode
PA23 7UH

Above *The small harbour at Toward*

Left *Toward Point lighthouse*

that sits behind it. There are three slipways at the club, two directly into the sea facing south and one inside the protection of the harbour wall. Part of the club premises lie on top of what was the swimming pool for the castle.

Toward is a very strategic location, with Rothesay on the Isle of Bute just a mile across the water to the west and the Scottish shore just three miles to the east.

An Caladh

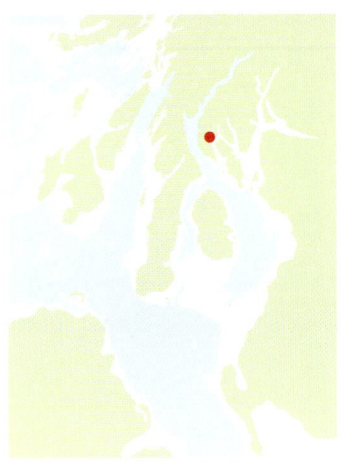

History and comments

An Caladh is a true hidden harbour, a sheltered bay with narrow channels marking the two entrances and an anchorage that is only revealed once inside. The small bay is protected by the uninhabited island of Eilean Dubh, which leaves it sheltered on all sides. It is a magical spot with very few signs of development and it strikes a marked contrast to Port Driseach, which is just along the coast towards Tighnabruaich. Although in the summer An Caladh is a very popular and often crowded anchorage.

The harbour remained fairly isolated until World War II, when it was used as a training base for landing craft crews and for the X-craft, which were based at nearby Port Bannatyne on the Isle of Bute.

The old launching slipway and boathouse

A slipway was installed along with a number of buildings onshore, which supplemented the old boathouse.

Today, an old stone quay remains, equipped with its original hand operated crane. There was once a large house along the shore, which had been taken over by the military during the war but this has since been demolished and only a section of its gardens remain. Other buildings on the shore are now being restored and it looks as though they will be used as holiday homes but their style is sympathetic and they do not impose on the dramatic landscape. How long this will remain the case is uncertain, as plans have been submitted for new developments.

A useful guide for the southern entrance to An Caladh is the old lighthouse, painted white, which lies on the spit of rocks marking the entrance.

This was established to mark the main outside channel but today it is just a beacon with no light, although the window where the light once shone out is still there. The former lighthouse keeper's cottage is one of the buildings that has been restored and turned into a holiday home. The northern entrance is marked by a smaller white stone beacon on a rock.

Along the coast to the west is Port Driseach where there is a messy boatyard that does little to complement the scenery. Fortunately, it is quite well hidden and has a small slipway for bringing boats out of the water, which is protected by stone breakwaters. You can drive as far as the boatyard but after this the road along the shore to An Caladh is private, so it is necessary to continue on foot.

Access by road
From Tighnabruaich, follow the shore road to the east until you reach the boatyard. Continue on foot along the single-track shore road for about a mile.

Parking
In the road before the boatyard.

Water access
Entering the harbour from either end is straightforward, although the northern channel is quite narrow. The deeper water in the bay lies towards the island and a considerable area on the land side dries out at low water.

Facilities
None in the surroundings of the bay but small town facilities in nearby Tighnabruaich.

Further information
www.visitscotland.com
www.kylesofbute.com

The restored quay and hand crane

The beautiful old lighthouse at the entrance

Kames

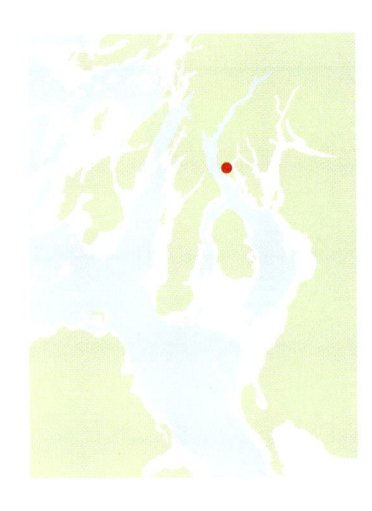

History and comments

The village of Kames is overshadowed by its larger neighbour, Tighnabruaich, and the two villages more or less merge into one another along the seafront road. Kames has always been the more commercial of the two harbours, whilst Tighnabruaich was the stopping off place for the steamer tourists.

The two piers at Kames were built to allow ships to come alongside and load the gunpowder that was produced by the factory just inland at Millhouse. This was known as the Kames Gunpowder Mill and its location is marked by a cairn on which one of the mortars used to test the gunpowder is mounted. A horse-drawn tramway was built to take the raw materials and the finished products to and from the pier. This facility was established in the mid 19th century and later, when steam power was used in the gunpowder mills, the coal came in by ship. Production at the gunpowder mills ceased in 1921 but the piers continued to be used by the Puffers for cargo and by a few fishing boats. In more recent times, the buildings around the piers were sold for conversion into private houses and today there is no land access to the two piers without the private access via these houses. Before this development the piers were in use by local fishermen.

The two private piers at Kames

The southern pier constructed with the classic vertical stones

Despite the challenging land access to the piers, Kames is still an interesting place to visit. The south pier is built of stone, whilst the longer northern pier has the stone construction at its landward end and wooden piling to form the outer end. For visiting yachts there is anchorage offshore, with tender landing on the beach.

To the south there is also an old stone slipway that looks as though it was a landing for fishermen and further south again is a newer slipway that can be used for boat launching and recovery. The latter is used by the Tighnabruaich Sailing School whose premises are just inland at Carry Farm.

Dominating the area around the piers at Kames is the Kames Hotel, which has 15 moorings available for visiting yachts that patronise the hotel.

Access by road
Follow the B8000 south from Tighnabruaich, at the cross roads by the village store turn left down the hill to the Kames Hotel.

Parking
Limited parking along the road or at the hotel.

Water access
The white painted hotel acts as a guide into Kames. No offshore dangers.

Facilities
The hotel and a village store/Post Office.

Further information
Kames Hotel ☎ 01700 811489
www.kames-hotel.com

Postcode
PA21 2AF

Otter Ferry

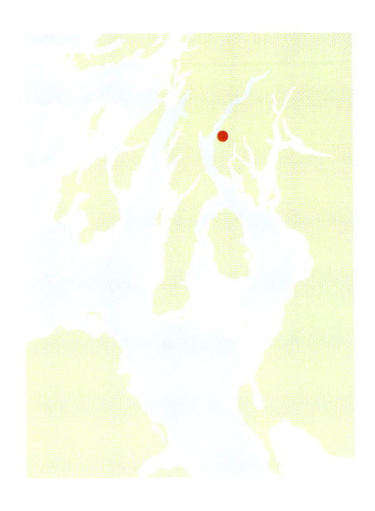

The Oystercatcher pub is the main attraction at Otter Ferry

History and comments

Otter Ferry is one of the wilder and more remote harbours in this book. Located on the shores of Loch Fyne, the longest of the southern lochs, Otter Ferry is served by a long and winding road along the shores of the loch from the north and an equally long road off the hills from the south. Despite its apparent remoteness, Otter Ferry is just an hour and a half away from Glasgow by road, demonstrating the extent to which this part of the highlands has been opened up by good roads.

In the past it was the water routes that provided the key to accessing this challenging terrain and Otter Ferry was part of a chain of ferries that provided links out to the Western Shores. The ferry service cut out the long land route across the mountains in the days when road travel was still a challenge, providing a shortcut both for passengers and for the sheep that were brought to market from the Kintyre Pensular. On the far side of the loch is another small harbour, known as West Otter Ferry, which was the ferry's western terminus. The two small harbours were built from local stone in around 1700 and were used by the ferry until 1948 when the service was closed down. They curve out from the shore in an L-shape.

During the war Loch Fyne could be closed off by a boom across the water from the spit and the foundations of the boom bases are just visible on shore near the spit. On the west shore the pier is now crumbling at its end and the old ferry building is derelict. At the eastern end, however, you will find the Oystercatcher pub which has become a destination for both yachtsmen and land tourists. The harbour here is well protected by the long shingle spit, with a boy marking its eastern end, that runs out into the loch to the south of the harbour. It is this shingle spit, rather than the animal, that gives the place its name; the word *oitir* means shingle spit or sandbank in Gaelic.

The harbour dries out completely at low water but the pub owners have provided a summer pontoon for yacht tenders and there are visitors' moorings too. The use of these facilities is free but a contribution towards upkeep is appreciated.

Access by road
The B8000 road runs along the eastern shore of the loch and passes Otter Ferry.

Parking
On the hard standing in front of the pub

Water access
Round the buoy marking the end of the spit. The white pub building is a clear guide into the moorings.

Facilities
The Oystercatcher pub and a nearly-built *bothy* with showers and toilets.

More information
www.otterferry.co.uk
Oystercatcher ☏ 01700 821229

Postcode
PA21 2DH

The tiny harbour, which marks one end of the ferry's route across the loch

Inveraray

History and comments

Inveraray is a major tourist town located towards the head of Loch Fyne and whilst it is the centre of this region its harbour seems to be taking a back seat. The town's main attraction is the remarkable castle just inland from the waters of the loch, the ancestral home of the Duke of Argyll.

The town itself was founded in 1745. The harbour at Inveraray was built at around the same time and used to bring in a lot of the building materials for the castle and the town but the harbour's main purpose was as the base for the herring fishing boats, which exploited the huge shoals of herring in the loch.

The harbour lies at a natural land formation that sticks out into the loch. It forms a natural breakwater, which was used as a harbour and fishing boat base long before the castle and town were built. The Duke of Argyll built the pier out into the loch to enclose a considerable area of water but most of this dries out with the tide and access is only at the pier head at low water.

When the Glasgow steamers started to operate up Loch Fyne in the 19th century a wooden extension of the pier was built out into the deeper water of the loch, enabling the steamers to come alongside at most states of tide. It was a bustling port that supplied the needs of the town and brought in visitors and cargo as well as serving as the base for the fishing fleet.

Sadly today the harbour is a shadow of its former self. The piers remain, of course, but apart from a few summer visitors it is only home to a floating museum that comprises two ships: the *Arctic Penguin*, a three-masted sailing ship and the *Vital Spark*, one of the few remaining Clyde Puffers. The *Arctic Penguin* is up for sale and the museum is closed with the pier looking to be in a sad condition but the harbour is still viable for visiting yachts if they can dry out at low tide.

Access by road

Inveraray lies on the main loch-side road, the A83.

Parking

Pay and display parking in the town and at the pier.

Water access

Straight up Loch Fyne with the white houses and the tower on the hill as a location guide. Anchorage possible to the north of the pier.

Facilities

All the facilities of a small town, including restaurants, cafés and pubs/hotels.

Further information

www.inveraraypier.com
inveraray-argyll.com

Postcode

PA32 8UY

The old stone cross on the quay at Inveraray, which dates from 1400 and was moved from the old village

Top left *The Clyde Puffer and the Arctic Penguin alongside at Inveraray*

Bottom left *The stone pier is now closed to the public*

Furnace

History and comments

The name gives something of a clue as to the origins of this village and harbour. It is unusual to find a remote village in the West Highlands with such an industrial past but Furnace has been home to three main industries over the years and it remains an active industrial base.

The first business to arrive was the Duddon company from Cumbria. In 1755 they established the iron furnace that gave the village its name. The business mined ore in Cumbria and was attracted to Furnace by the plentiful supplies of charcoal from the local forests, which were needed for smelting.

The furnace was shut down in 1828 but the charcoal supply was also responsible for the next industry that arrived in Furnace, the manufacture of gunpowder. The powder works was established in 1841 but was closed down again in 1883 after an 80-ton storage unit blew up, raising serious safety concerns.

The quarry, Furnace's third industry, was established in 1841, at the same time as the gunpowder works and presumably used their products to exploit the red granite rock. Much of this was shipped out to Glasgow in the form of the

Stone from the quarry was used to extend the pier

Modern industrial equipment now dominates the pier

The pier is no longer used to ship out stone

granite setts used on the city's streets. Unlike its neighbour Crarae, just down the road, this quarry is still in operation today, although on a much smaller scale and no longer supplying granite setts. Breedon, which now operates the site, is principally a supplier of ready mixed concrete and asphalt and the harbour is no longer used, except by divers.

The harbour was built out into the loch using stones from the quarry. On its west side there is a vertical stone wall and to the east a small wooden quay structure where the ships could come alongside for loading. In its original form, when sailing ships would bring in the iron ore, this would have been a busy dock area. Now it appears that the products from the quarry all leave by road rather than by sea. The village's newest industry is fish farming. Aquaculture has established a fish farm just to the east of the harbour and a hatchery on land just to the harbour's west. The village itself is now principally residential and does not have a lot to offer the visitor.

Access by road
Furnace lies just off the A83 coast road on a turning to the left when coming from the north. There is no easy access to the harbour area except by foot along the shore.

Parking
Roadside parking.

Water access
No off-lying dangers and the possibility of an anchorage to the SW of the harbour area with beach landing.

Facilities
A pub and a Post Office/store in the village.

Further information
Breedon Aggregates ☎ 01499 500268

Postcode
PA32 8XW

Crarae

History and comments

The quarry that overlooks the village of Crarae, on the western side of Loch Fyne, was established in the 18th century to produce the quality granite of the hillside, most of which was dressed and shaped before being loaded onto a stone jetty built out from the shore and shipped to Glasgow. The quarry at Crarae was renowned for its annual explosion, organised to dislodge the thousands of tons of rock required to keep the quarry men going for the rest of the year. Located in the side of a steeply rising hill, holes were drilled well into the rock and packed with seven tons of explosives. The spectacular explosion that this created became a tourist attraction.

One year, unfortunately, it went tragically wrong. The explosion had been timed to take place when an excursion steamer from Glasgow, packed with 100 people, was watching offshore. The explosion successfully dislodged around 70,000 tons of rock in the blast. As the dust settled, many of the passengers from the steamer came ashore for a closer look and walked right into the quarry. Tragically, the

The crumbling old quarry quay with the fish farm beyond

The fish farm pier is used to land visitors to the nearby gardens

explosion had released a cloud of poisonous gas, which left many unconscious and seven dead from the exposure.

The quarry has now closed down and is the sheltered site of the famed Crarae Gardens, filled with exotic plants. The stone jetty is falling into disrepair and has been replaced, a little further to the south, by a slipway and a floating pontoon that provides the landing point for the large fish farm located just offshore. Passengers disembarking from small visiting cruise ships to visit the Crarae Gardens also use the slipway and there is a small boatyard on the shore.

The slipway and old jetty are well hidden from the road and public access in not encouraged. A small garden centre is located at the roadside by the new piers and this, along with the trees planted along the shore, hides the shore-based facilities of the fish farm. The village of Crarae is some half a mile to the south of these jetties.

Access by road
The main loch-side road, the A83 runs past the jetty site.

Parking
There is an unmarked one car lay-by on the loch side that can give foot access to the old stone quay. The garden centre has a good car park for customers but visitors are not encouraged to venture further along the track to the jetties.

Water access
Very straightforward up the loch but if you plan to go ashore on the pontoon jetty, be aware that there is a floating barrier heading out from the shore to connect to the fish farm, so you will have to enter the area from the northeast, around the fish farm.

Facilities
Tea rooms at the garden centre.

Further information
Quarry View Garden Centre ☎ 01546 886692

Postcode
PA32 8YA

The modern slipway with the old quay in the distance

Lochgair

History and comments

Lochgair, situated on the west side of Loch Fyne, is a mini-loch with a relatively narrow entrance forming a natural harbour on the southern shores of Loch Fyne. It is, therefore, surprising that is has not been developed more than it has. It retains a wonderful rural atmosphere with minimal modern development along its shores. There is a small hydro-electric power station on the shore that gets its power from a loch high in the hills but this is well hidden by trees and does not intrude on the landscape.

The shores of the loch are shallow beaches virtually all round, although there is a house right on the shore on the western side with a stone wall along its loch side edge. This gives it the appearance of having been a small quay in the past and it would have been a logical place for landing supplies to the small village before road transport was developed.

Just inshore from the house are further buildings that have the appearance of old fishermen's cottages and there are signs of the small scale fishing and agriculture that were the main reasons for the existence of the village in the past.

Further round on the south side of the enclosed loch you will find a private slipway leading into the loch. If you follow this around, there is a vehicle

On the water's edge, this house occupies what was probably a quay in the past

ford and a footbridge across a stream with a path leading out to the castle at the south entrance point of the loch. It seems that although this castle has a similar appearance to many of the ancient castles along the shores of the Scottish lochs, it was in fact built as a look out around the beginning of the 18th century, suggesting that the loch was being used as a harbour in those days. Today, the castle is a private residence but it makes for a useful guide to the entrance.

Although the loch has retained its peaceful and undeveloped atmosphere you can't help feeling that it is ripe for development but for now it is a peaceful and popular anchorage where yachts can lie afloat for a trip ashore to the welcoming Lochgair Hotel on the main road.

Access by road
The village and loch lie on the main A83 coast road.

Parking
There is parking at the hotel and in a lay-by on the main road. Limited parking in the village.

Water access
The castle and a white house on the southern point of the entrance provide a guide in. There are no dangers in the loch, except for the shallow shore beaches.

Facilities
Lochgair Hotel on the main road provides food and drink.

Further information
Lochgair Hotel www.lochgairhotel.com

Postcode
PA31 8SA

Old buildings on the water's edge at Lochgair

The private slipway and, in the distance, the pedestrian bridge that gives access over the ford at high water

Carradale

History and comments

Carradale and Carradale East merge together to form one large village but the harbour is definitely located in Carradale East. It is tucked into the lee of a promontory that juts out into Kilbrannan Sound and can be quite exposed in southerly winds, although the island of Arran creates good shelter to the east. It was this exposure and the desire to provide better weather protection that led to the construction of the current harbour.

Carradale East was a small fishing community whose boats operated off the beach and fished for herring. Then, in the early 19th century, steamers started to call in on their way to Campbeltown, which led to the building of the first wooden pier at the harbour in 1858. This was replaced in 1870 with the first iron pier to be built in Scotland. This had two levels, an upper one on the outside of the pier for the steamers and a lower one on the inside of the head of the pier for the fishing boats.

The steamers' use of the harbour led to Carradale's development as a holiday resort and the place soon began to thrive but the pier's exposure to the wind and seas funnelling up from the south was a handicap and once the steamer trade started to decline in the

The rough and ready finish to the pier at Carradale

1950s the time was ripe for redevelopment of the harbour.

This took place around 1960 when construction of the current harbour took place. The elegant lines of the iron pier were replaced by the rather brutal steel pile construction of the new one. This curved around almost in a semi-circle, starting out heading to the north as it left the land and ending up heading west. It is a solid pier with steel piling edges filled with stone and it provides excellent shelter for the small fleet of fishing boats that now use the harbour. Leisure use is encouraged and a slipway has been constructed in the harbour for boat launching but the harbour is small and space limited.

Carradale is somewhat off the beaten track on the east side of the Mull of Kintyre and it is trying to attract more tourists and visiting yachts.

Access by road
From Tarbet to the north take the A83 south and then turn left onto the B842. This road bypasses the village, so watch for the turn off signs.

Parking
Ample free parking at the harbour.

Water access
Easy access from seaward but stay close to the harbour wall when entering as shallow water is only a short way off. It is possible to moor alongside but check with the harbour master.

Facilities
All the facilities of a large village, including several hotels, a shop, garage and a Post Office

Further information
www.carradaleharbour.co.uk
Harbourmaster (located at Campbeltown)
stephen.scally@argyll-bute.gov.uk
☏ 01586 552552

Postcode
PA28 6RY

The harbour at Carradale resurrected with a steel pile pier

The harbour facilities at Carradale encourage leisure use

Blackwaterfoot

History and comments

Blackwaterfoot must be one of the smallest harbours on record; it is no more than 30 metres across and only slightly longer. Beautifully formed, it has been dug out from the river bank and lined with well executed stonework. It might seem strange to have constructed such a harbour on the western side of the island of Arran, which, despite gaining some protection from the Kintyre Peninsula several miles to the west, remains fairly exposed, however, the harbour was built when land transport was still a challenge and access by water was vital.

With room for just a few boats, Blackwaterfoot is one of the smallest harbours on record

When you analyse the size of the harbour you realise that it has been built to allow just enough space for a 20 metre long Clyde Puffer to enter, moor alongside and then turn and leave, bow first, using the flow of the water coming down the river. Blackwaterfoot is likely, therefore, to have been built to allow delivery by Clyde Puffer of materials, such as coal, to the village and the surrounding areas. You have to admire the construction: the grassy banks of the harbour lead up to a beautiful stone bridge accros the River Blackwater, just beyond which is a weir that helps to control the flow of water.

You get the impression that the harbour's current surroundings have been landscaped to help create the setting for the relatively modern hotel that dominates the area to the south of the harbour. A few local boats, probably used for angling trips, use the harbour. They are moored away from the stone wall, suggesting that you may get a swell coming into the harbour at high water. The harbour entrance is between the sandbanks of the river entrance but some attempt has been made to stabilise these with stone breakwaters on the south side, which are covered at high water. The granite mooring posts remain and the harbour is now something of a tourist attraction.

The weir that controls the water flow into the harbour

Access by road
From the ferry at Brodick, take the A880 over the hills direct to Blackwaterfoot.

Parking
Between the hotel and the harbour.

Water access
The white hotel building provides a good indication of where the entrance lies, it is then straight in with the bridge as a guide. Beware of the stone breakwaters on the south side, which are covered at high water. The entrance channel is marked by unpainted poles.

Facilities
Hotel and shop.

Further information
Blackwaterfoot Harbour Association, Harbour House, Blackwaterfoot.

Postcode
KA27 8EZ

Gigha

The old rock-enclosed harbour near the ferry slipway

Gigha ferry on the Tayinloan side

History and comments

Tayinloan is the ferry terminal on the mainland that connects to the island of Gigha, two miles offshore. At Tayinloan there are two piers, a substantial one that serves as the current ferry terminal and, slightly further north, the old ferry terminal, which was used when smaller ferries operated on the route. The direct ferry to Gigha has only operated since 1979. Before this the ferry to Islay would stop off on its way to the outer island.

Over on the Gigha side, the ferry terminal is a concrete ramp laid out over the rocks but close alongside to the south of this ramp is one of the original harbours of Gigha. Gallochoille is little more than a sandy beach that dries out at low water and which is partly protected by a rough stone breakwater. Today it serves as a harbour for small angling and fishing boats, whilst the main harbour is a group of moorings just to the south at Ardminish. These moorings are served by small pier, running out from the shore, that serves as a tender landing place. At the time of writing a floating pontoon was being installed here to make landing available at all states of tide.

Further to the south is the substantial South Pier, used as a landing point for cargoes, the night lay up berth for the ferry, and a base for larger fishing boats.

Gigha is, therefore, well served by harbours and the remains of further small harbours with stone piers are dotted around the island's coastline, serving as relics of the past.

The history of Gigha goes back thousands of years to a time when, thanks to the relative ease of their defence, islands were favoured places to live. Today the island has a population of about 200 and is owned by the community as part of a pioneering project. Visitors are encouraged because they help to support the island's economy, which is principally based on tourism, farming and fishing, hence the pontoon for visiting yachts.

Moorings can be difficult to find as they tend to be permanently occupied but there is reasonably sheltered anchorage further offshore and in the sheltered bay to the north of the ferry terminal.

Access by road

The village of Tayinloan lies on the main A83 coast road and the ferry terminal is well signposted from there. The ferry runs at frequent intervals throughout the day.

Parking

There is parking at the ferry terminal at Tayinloan and plenty on Gigha.

Water access

There are rocky outcrops in the channel between Gigha and the mainland but these are well marked from both the north and the south.

Facilities

There are good facilities on Gigha, including guesthouses, a pub and a shop/Post Office. On the Tayinloan side is Big Jessie's tea room.

Further information

Ferry times www.calmac.co.uk
www.gigha.org.uk

Postcode

Tayinloan PA29 6XQ

The main mooring area at Gigha where a new pontoon is being installed

Keillmore

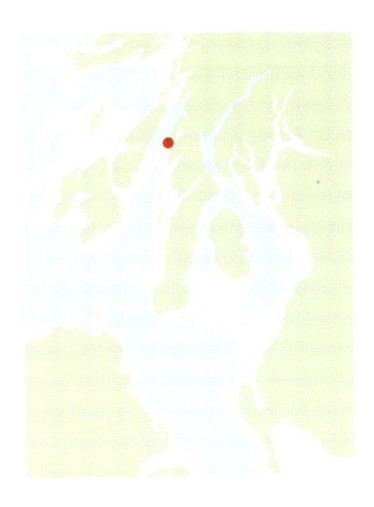

History and comments

Keillmore lies in a strategic location at the northern side of the promontory between Loch Sween and the Sound of Luing. It is the closest point between the mainland and the island of Jura so it comes as no surprise that it was originally the location for a ferry service across the sound. The ferry service from Keillmore was established in 1817 with the construction of the old pier in a small creek on the west side of the Keillmore peninsula.

The rough stone pier must have presented a challenge to the sailors who tried to get their ships alongside. The rock-strewn creek is narrow and twisting and the pier, which is no longer connected to the track that provided its access, is falling into disrepair. A later pier was built in the creek closer to the sea. It is in the form of a slipway, which must have made it much easier to unload the cattle that were transported across from Jura. The slipway pier is to the south of the old pier and is also constructed of loose stones. Access to this later pier must still have required considerable seamanship to bring the ferry in whilst avoiding the rocky reefs lying close offshore.

The ferry service was finally closed down early in the 20th century when Clyde Puffers took over the transport from Jura to ports on the mainland coast that were easier to access.

There is a newer pier on the east side of the Keillmore promontory that runs out into deeper water. It was probably used by larger vessels delivering supplies to this remote location. Today it is visited by the occasional yacht and is used by fishing boats but there are no facilities onshore.

Despite its remote location at the end of the road, Keillmore attracts visitors to its ancient chapel, the Keills Chapel, on the hillside above the newest pier. The chapel dates back to the 12th century and is open to the public with its collection of old gravestones and a Celtic cross.

The new slipway landing

The modern pier on the south side is a safe landing point but there are no facilities here

To visit the old piers on the west side, there is a winding single-track road across the promontory, over the hill and down to the shore. The road is narrow and gated, offering no passing places and only a small turning area at the pier; its use is, therefore, not encouraged and walking is the best option.

Access by road
A long single-track road south from Tayvallich, an extension of the B8025.

Parking
Very limited parking at the south pier and at the gate across the road.

Water access
Challenging navigation into the old piers but straightforward at the new pier to the south. Here there is space to anchor but it is a bit exposed to the southwest.

Facilities
None

Postcode
PA31 8PX

The original pier at Keillmore is being restored

Tayvallich

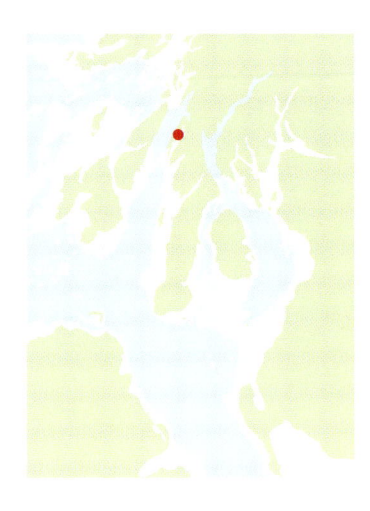

History and comments

There has been a settlement at Tayvallich for thousands of years thanks to the sheltered harbour, which gives safe sea access, and the surrounding land that is suitable for agriculture. Located close to the head of Loch Sween, this harbour is one of the most sheltered in the Western Isles, with the water area completely enclosed except for a narrow entrance between the rocky outcrops. It is almost the perfect harbour but the water is quite shallow on the northern side; most of the mooring and activity is, therefore, located in the southern half of the harbour. Several private jetties, with pontoons at their ends, reach out into the harbour and a stone jetty, probably dating back hundreds of years, has now been restored and serves, principally, as a landing point for the local fishing boats.

The new pier and pontoons that provide the terminus for the ferry at Jura

HIDDEN HARBOURS OF SOUTHWEST SCOTLAND

Two beacons mark the narrow entrance to the harbour

Fishing has long been an important part of the local economy and several fishing boats continue to operate from the harbour, mainly fishing for shellfish.

The recently started ferry service that provides a passenger-only link with the island of Jura runs from Tayvallich. Along with the terminal on the waterfront, the council has built a pontoon with several finger berths where yachts can moor temporarily. The ferry crossing takes under an hour to make the crossing down Loch Sween and across the Sound of Jura. It runs just twice a day, from April to the end of September.

The rocky ridges that enclose the harbour entrance are virtually covered at high water so you need to identify the entrance markers before making the commitment to enter the narrow channel between the rocks. The are two entrances between these rocks and the first one you come to is not the one you want; this makes the markers on the rocks even more important.

It is interesting that a harbour that has been in use for such a long time has so little in the way of history on show but despite being a small village, seemingly dedicated to the sea, there are good facilities onshore that make it well worth a visit, although things do tend to close down in the winter. There is a sailing school plus a hotel, a shop and a café. Outside the entrance, if you head further north up the very narrow loch to Scotnish, there are a couple of old private stone piers.

The old fisherman's jetty

Access by road
From the south bank of the Crinan Canal take the B8025. This road eventually reaches Tayvallich.

Parking
Along the road.

Water access
From Loch Sween turn around the square headland as the harbour comes into view and then identify the beacons marking the narrow entrance. Beware of further rocks inside the harbour area. There are marked visitor moorings and an anchorage around the patch of rocks in the harbour.

Facilities
A hotel, pub, café and shop.

Further information
Tayvallich Bay Association www.tayvallich.com

Postcode
PA31 4BE

Achnamara

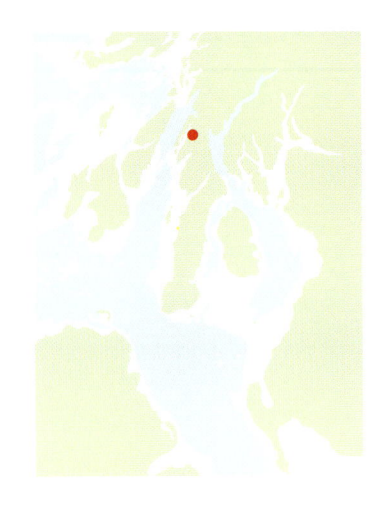

The idyllic anchorage at Achnamara

History and comments

Achnamara is one of the smallest of our hidden harbours, tucked away on a small loch that branches off Loch Sween, near its top end. It is a delightfully remote spot, open to the southwest but with a couple of islands that shelter the moorings from the prevailing wind. It is located several miles up a single-track road that does not lead anywhere significant beyond the village so its peace and quiet is guaranteed.

Today it is mainly is used as a peaceful mooring for yachts but in the past it played host to cargo ships, both sail and steam. A reminder of this past activity is found in the stone pier located along the shores of the loch to the southwest of the village and alongside the road that runs along the edge of the loch. A parking area occupies the spot that was once the site of a small building for checking the incoming cargoes. Stretching out into the loch from here is the pier. It was constructed from rocks laid vertically; a style found in other old Scottish piers and thought to have been pioneered by Thomas Telford, the engineer who was responsible for building many of the bridges and piers in this part of Scotland in the early part of the 18th century.

The pier at Achnamara was used to bring in cargoes of coal and other supplies for the large houses of the region's estates. The whole area is heavily forested and one of the main exports sent out from the pier was, therefore, timber. It is thought that the pier was last used commercially in around 1950 when a Clyde Puffer called and today it is used as a tender landing site for yachts moored offshore. This pier lies about half a mile from the village but closer in there is a small pontoon pier, seemingly privately constructed, used for tender landing.

The village is tiny, more of a hamlet, with just twenty-four properties, one of them an abandoned school that was used as a youth outdoor activities centre for 30 years up until 1997.

Access by road

Take the B8025 from alongside the Crinan Canal and turn onto a single-track road signposted to Achnamara.

Parking
Limited parking at the pier.

Water access
Straightforward. Up the loch, passing to the north of the small island just before the pier. There is a patch of rocks just to the north of the pier but adequate water inside them.

Facilities
None

Further information
Achnamara Mooring Association

Postcode
PA31 8PX

The stone pier provides a landing point but there are no facilities on shore

The traditional vertical stone construction of the pier

Craighouse

History and comments

Craighouse is known for being incredibly challenging to get to. By car this is certainly true, as the journey requires two ferry crossings and miles of single-track road. By sea, however, it is far simpler. The harbour is just a short hop across the Sound of Jura from the mainland and benefits from good facilities to welcome visiting yachtsmen.

Craighouse occupies a protected position on the east coast of Jura, further sheltered from the east and south by the Small Isles, and has been the island's main harbour over the centuries. The old stone pier here curves out from the shore and was originally used for bringing in stores and mooring fishing boats. However, in the early 20th century a piled pier was built to the south to serve as a terminal for a ferry service to the mainland. This ferry service has long since closed down but the pier remains in good condition and is now used mainly by fishing boats.

There is a direct ferry service to Craighouse in the summer months, operated by a passenger-only RIB. If you want to bring a car you must first go to Islay and then take another ferry across to Jura.

The old harbour with the 'new' steamer pier in the distance

Jura distillery is the main employer for the island's 200 residents and dominates Craighouse. In the past the stone pier was used to bring in the raw materials required for the distillery's whisky production. The modern distillery was reopened in 1963 and, in addition to producing sought-after whiskies, is now a visitor attraction.

Until recently, the old stone pier at Craighouse was largely abandoned and used only by the local fishing boats but it now serves as the base for a floating pontoon that extends from its end to create a landing place for visiting yachts and the RIB ferry. Visiting yachts are important to the economy and are welcomed with 16 deep-water moorings offshore and additional space to anchor. Further north at Lagg there are the remains of a stone pier that was used for shipping cattle across to the mainland, connecting with the old stone piers at Keills. Despite its remote location, Craighouse has become a good yachting destination, and in recognition of its positive effect on the island's economy, considerable investment has been made in its facilities.

Access by road
The single-track A846 follows the coast from the ferry terminal on the west side of Jura.

Parking
Roadside parking.

Water access
From the south, via the marked channel inside the Small Isles and from the north, inside the islands parallel to the shore.

Facilities
The Jura Hotel and a shop/Post Office. Showers and toilets for yachts. Whisky tasting.

Further information
Jura Development Trust ☏ 01496 820161

Postcode
PA26 7XU

The original stone pier at Craighouse

The distillery is the focal point of the village

Port Charlotte and Bruinladdich

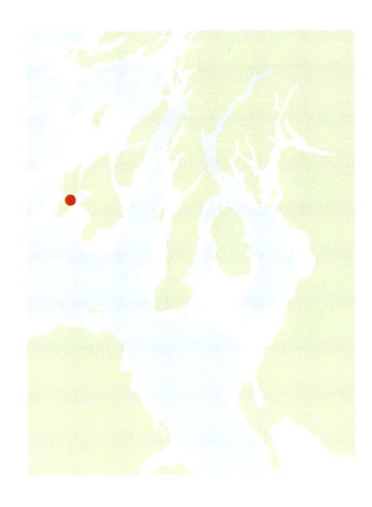

History and comments

Although a couple of miles apart, these two harbours on the island of Islay are closely related. The area around Loch Indaal is in the heart of Islay whisky country and both villages have distilleries, although the one at Port Charlotte is not currently operating. Loch Indaal is a deep inlet running in from the sea on the south west coast of Islay and its mouth is wide open to the Atlantic. A visit is not, therefore, to be taken lightly in adverse weather conditions.

The history of both villages is closely related to their distilleries. The one at Bruinladdich opened in 1881 and closed down in 1994. It was re-opened in 2000 and is reported to be doing well. The owners of the distillery have now bought some of the warehouse buildings of the distillery in Port Charlotte and there is talk of reopening this distillery too. The expansion of both Port Charlotte and Bruichladdich from small fishing communities into villages can be largely attributed to the presence of the distilleries. Housing was built for the workers and stone piers were constructed to provide landing points for the ships that brought in barley for the factories; the sacks of barley were then transported to the distillery by pony and cart.

The breakwater at Port Charlotte with Indaal lighthouse in the distance

Today Port Charlotte is a tourist resort with a hotel, guest houses and a good beach. The stone pier remains much as it was and provides shelter to a few summer boats. It is also a landing point for the tenders of any yachts anchoring offshore. In Bruichladdich the old pier was extended and modernised in 2004 with eight dolphins and associated walkways. It can now accommodate the large, modern, double hull tankers that bring in fuel for Gleaner Oils at the Gleaner depot to the north of the piers. Previously only small tankers could berth alongside the old stone pier.

Unlike many places covered by this book, there are no moorings here for visiting yachts. Although there are enough facilities onshore to make a visit worthwhile, this south coast of Islay is a little off the main cruising routes and the small marina at Bowmore seems to be a more attractive alternative.

Access by road
After leaving the ferry at Port Ellen, follow the A846 coast road around the edge of the loch to the west side.

Parking
On-street parking.

Water access
The route into Loch Indaal is straightforward with Indaal lighthouse, which lies between the two harbours providing a guide. Anchor offshore.

Facilities
Hotels, shops, Post Office and cafés are all available.

Further information
Martin Gorringe at Argyll and Bute Council handles all harbour enquiries.
martin.gorringe@argyll-bute.gov.uk

Postcode
Port Charlotte PA48 7TX
Bruinladdich PA49 7UN

A section of the modern oil tanker pier

The distilleries are the focal point of both villages

Portnahaven

History and comments

This southwest corner of Islay is wide open to the Atlantic and its importance as a landfall point for inbound ships is shown by the impressive lighthouse located on a small island offshore. It is the offshore islands that render the small harbour at Portnahaven viable, as they break up the power of the Atlantic storms. However, the absence of jetties or wharves in the harbour implies that the Atlantic swell still reaches into the area. Just around the corner from the harbour area, facing the exposed southwest, is the world's first, operational, wave-power station, which has been producing the power for the island since 2000.

There has been a settlement of fishermen and crofters on the offshore island of Orsay since 1300 but Portnahaven was only developed in the 18th century, when crofters were cleared from the inland farming areas and settled here. Fishing was an

Moorings in the harbour. The lighthouse is situated on one of the offshore islands

Whitewashed cottages line the harbour

important activity, benefitting from the village's location close to offshore waters. Much of the fish was dried and sent across the water to Ireland and it has been suggested that in the past Portnahaven had more contact with Ireland than with the Scottish mainland. Today, however, everything comes by road via the ferry to Port Ellen.

Nowadays, Portnahaven's main activity is tourism and many of the cottages are second homes. It is an active village with a pub and a shop and out on the eastern headland there is a small boatyard with a slipway for hauling up boats for repair and storage. This is also the location of the one small quay in the harbour. The boatyard does not appear to be very active; some of the boats on land look as though they will never go to sea again. There are still a few fishing boats using the harbour but they are small potting boats. Nextdoor neighbour Port Wemyss is a similar but much smaller inlet and the name suggests that it was a harbour, although it has very limited boating activity these days. Both harbours are noted for the white-washed cottages that line the harbours and for the seals that are regular visitors.

Access by road
Take the A847 single track road. It is an extension of the main road in Islay from the ferry terminal.

Parking
Roadside parking.

Water access
Take the channel inside the offshore islands from either the east or the west, with anchorage off the harbour inlet. There are moorings inside the harbour but these are occupied by local boats.

Facilities
A pub and a shop/Post Office.

More information
None available.

Postcode
PA47 7SJ

Slipways at the boatyard

Toberonchy

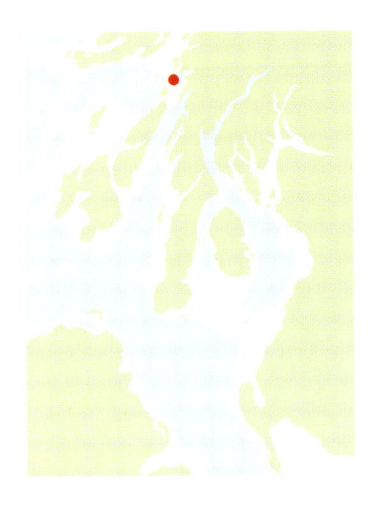

A wooden mooring post on the slate beach

History and comments

When you enter Toberonochy these days it is hard to believe that this was once a thriving quarrying community. Today the village is a quiet, rural island retreat with stunning views out over the water but close to two centuries ago work started on quarrying the slate for which the island of Luing is famous. The quarry was located to the south and west of the existing village and still exists although it is largely hidden from view. The most visible remnant of the slate activity is the harbour from which the slate was shipped out to Glasgow and many other parts of the globe. It is estimated that around 50,000 slates were produced here every week.

The two quays that constitute the present harbour were built of rubble from the quarry and the quay walls are faced with slate rocks. The main quay to the north of the inlet has been surfaced with concrete and the area behind has been grassed over but this is the area that was used for the slate production, the raw rocks being brought down from the quarry by tramway and then split and shaped by hand. The chippings can be clearly seen in the content of the beach which is like a form of black sand made from the slate chippings. The private island of Shuna offshore offers excellent protection for the harbour.

Slate production ceased here quite early on and the quarry was closed down in 1914. Looking at the houses in the village they are almost all of the style found in other mining villages; low, double room cottages. There are just two streets in the village, which was primarily built to house the miners.

Today the harbour is a quiet spot with two adjacent coves and picnic areas. There are mooring buoys offshore and it is a favoured anchorage for visiting yachts although there are no onshore facilities for them. The land around the harbour is now owned by the Latimers, who have been responsible for tidying up the area. An application to start a small shell fishing operation here has been turned down because of strong local pressure, although judging by the lobster pots on the quay some shell fishing is already taking place. At present, therefore, the peace and quiet remains.

Access by road

From the Cuan ferry follow the main road (single-track) south, signposted to Toberonochy.

The harbour was originally developed to ship out slate from the local quarry

The quay at Toberonchy has been restored

Parking
On the quay.

Water access
Up the Sound of Shuna with direct access into the harbour, which dries at low water.

Facilities
None

Further information
Hillary Latimer, landowner ☏ 0191 528 5235

Postcode
PA34 4UE

Arduaine

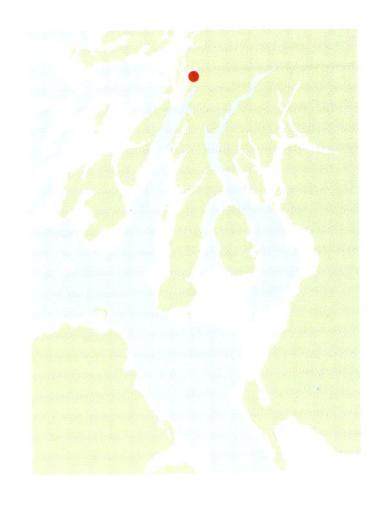

History and comments

Arduaine lies just north of Craobh Haven Marina and is probably by-passed by most yachts on their way north. There is little in the way of facilities, except for a very nice hotel that offers dramatic views over the sounds to the west but it is possible to find a peaceful anchorage here when you want to escape the close confinement of the nearby marina.

Arduaine boasts three piers around its headland location at the entrance to Loch Melfort, two of these are on the more sheltered north side and are dedicated to servicing nearby fish farms, the third has a long history as the landing place for boat services out to the island of Shuna, a couple of miles across the sound. Originally this pier was built from the local stone but it has been extended and surfaced with concrete and is not the prettiest pier in the world. It can be used by small craft at all states of

Fish farming is big business in this area

the tide and it is possible to anchor offshore here and land by tender for the short walk up to the hotel. There is also a sort of slipway alongside the pier where boats can be launched.

On the opposite side of the sound at Shuna there is a matching pier but this one is a bit more sophisticated, with a floating pontoon alongside.

Both piers were built in 1908 to allow materials for the building of the castle on the island to be transported across the sound. Today they are used to take guests across to the holiday homes located on the island and to transport supplies; the boats are kept at the more sheltered harbour on the island when not in use. Both piers are privately owned, as is the island, and landing is by invitation only.

The two fish farm piers are, of course, also private and their use as a landing point is not encouraged. Their location in the more sheltered waters of the north side might provide a better anchorage but beware of the extensive fish farming equipment offshore.

Access by road
Arduaine lies on the main A816 coast road.

Parking
There is parking at the Shuna Island slipway, just off the main road and parking at the hotel.

Water access
No major off-lying dangers apart from the fish farms.

Facilities
The Loch Melfort Hotel is open for meals and drinks. www.lochmelfort.co.uk

Further information
www.islandofshuna.co.uk
☏ 01852 314244

Postcode
PA34 4XQ

The 'modern' pier at Arduaine, which is the access point to the island of Shuna

Fish farm pier to the east of the headland

Melfort

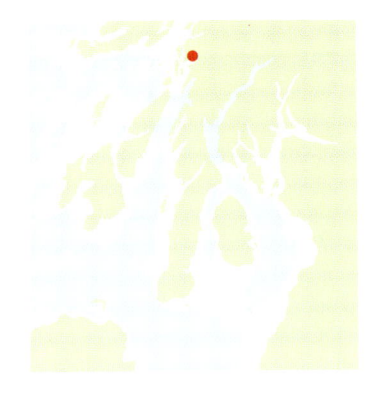

The old pier is now incorporated into the holiday home development

History and comments

It is hard to relate the current harbour at Melfort with an industrial past but back in the 19th century it was a centre for the manufacture of gunpowder for ammunition and quarrying. The remains of the old gunpowder factory are still visible to the east of Melfort House. It was connected to the pier by means of a horse drawn tramway used for bringing in raw materials. The local forests provided the oak wood needed for the manufacture of charcoal, which was in turn an essential ingredient in the manufacture of the gunpowder. Although the main gunpowder mill was established in the 19th century it is thought that there were earlier smaller mills in the area. A wood behind the village and close to Melfort House is still called Magazine Wood. The old stone pier is one of the few in the region that has access at all states of tide. It was used not only for the shipping in of raw materials for gunpowder and the shipping out of the finished product but also, like so many piers in this part of the highlands, to bring in all sorts of manufactured goods and coal and to ship out agricultural produce and timber. Sailing ships and subsequently the Clyde Puffers would have carried the cargo in and out and piers are a feature of many of the estates along the shores of Loch Melfort.

The old pier still remains but is now surrounded by a group of holiday homes that are mainly time shares. These prevent public access to the pier itself and form what is more or less a gated community. With the development of these properties a small harbour has been created to the east of the old pier. Boats up to 20 feet in length can access this enclosed harbour when the tide is right. Inside the new harbour there are floating pontoons and most of the facilities found in a modern marina but on a tiny scale. Visiting yachts can use moorings out in the bay and land by tender in the harbour. A few hundred yards along the shore there is another old pier. This is also being developed with holiday cottages alongside a small harbour that looks like it

The tiny harbour at the holiday home development

will be very similar to Melfort. It is a pity that there is not more public access to these areas but both harbours do seem to want to limit public access because of the lack of parking so unless you are on foot access is very limited.

Access by road
Heading south, take the turning onto a minor road signposted to Melfort. Follow this until the sign reading Melfort Harbour and Pier. This single-track road winds along the shore to the pier area.

Parking
Very limited once you approach the harbour area.

Water access
Easy access from the water to the moorings but access to the small harbour is tidal and available from about half tide onwards.

Facilities
The Shower of Herring restaurant in the village

Further information
www.melfortpier.com
www.melfortvillage.co.uk

Postcode
PA34 4XD

Cuan Ferry

History and comments

The island of Luing has a long and turbulent history and the ferry connecting the island to the neighbouring island of Seil has been an essential part of this history. Initially operated by rowing boats and later by steam and then internal combustion power, the ferry originally transported people but was subsequently used for ferrying cattle across the narrow straight. Today the ferry is a modern vessel capable of carrying up to six cars or one truck and it operates from concrete slipways off either side. These slipways are a relatively new addition and previously the ferry operated from small harbours and piers on either side. On the eastern side the harbour was enclosed by a stone, L-shaped pier but one arm of this has now been incorporated into the ferry slipway, meaning that the harbour is now formed by a stone pier jutting out from the side of the slipway. This harbour is used mainly by small fishing boats and virtually dries out at low water.

There are steps on the outer arm of the pier for landing. A second cove with a private pier lies a little to the north.

On the west side there are two coves and the ferry slipway now occupies the more southerly of these, whilst the north cove acts as a small harbour. Here

The old harbour on the mainland side

there are the remains of a stone pier and alongside this is a modern gangway and floating pontoon, which is now the base for the fishing boats that use this harbour. Further round to the south, where there is shelter from the prevailing wind, there is another jetty and landing places but these all appear to be private.

The waters through the narrow straight between the two islands have fierce currents which the ferry negotiates with considerable skill. These currents run at up to eight knots and there have been reports of standing waves in the tide race at certain times of tide. In a northerly gale this can be a challenging sound to negotiate, particularly with the rocks that extend out into the northern entrance to the channel. Although the sound runs from north to south the names cause some confusion because the western village is called South Cuan. There has been discussion about building a bridge across the sound but the high cost of the project is against it.

Access by road
The ferry is well signposted throughout the island of Seil and is located at the end of the main road that runs across the island.

Parking
Limited parking on both sides away from the ferry queue.

Water access
Access from both the north and the south ends of the sound. Marked rocks are a potential hazard at the north end.

Facilities
None

Further information
www.sailscotland.co.uk

Postcode
PA34 4TU

The pontoon landing stage on the Luing side

The ferry across the narrow strait

Ellenabeich and Easdale

History and comments

The village of Ellenabeich was at the centre of the slate quarrying industry, the trade that has been the mainstay of this region to the south of Oban for centuries. Indeed, the group of islands in this region are known as the Slate Islands and there are many quarries dotted around the coast. Ellenabeich, on the island of Seil, was the site of a huge slate quarry that had origins going back to the 1500s. The main quarry here at Ellenabeich was started in the mid 1700s and became a deep hole extending to 250 feet below sea level, with just a rock barrier separating it from the sea. As it got deeper it relied on steam pumps to keep the water at bay; coal was, therefore, an important import here. By 1870 the combined output of this quarry and those on the island of Easdale just across the water filled ten steamers every week. These were loaded from a wooden pier built out into the channel between Ellenabeich and the Island of Easdale. The pier still exists today, although only as a ruin, with no access from the land.

In 1881 a violent storm breached the wall around the Ellenabeich quarry and it was flooded. Production ceased and hundreds of jobs were lost, leading to a massive reduction in the harbour traffic. The same storm damaged the quarries on Easdale but these were pumped out again and remained in production for another 30 years.

The small harbour at Easdale, created from slate rubble

Today Ellenabeich is a tourist village, complete with a visitor centre, but the now small harbour retains its character. It is used mainly by fishing boats but it is also the departure point for the foot ferry across to Easdale Island, where there is another small harbour that acts as the south terminus. There is a small, slate-built waiting room for the ferry in each harbour. Ellenabeich harbour is also the base for RIB tours of the islands and nearby channels, with their dramatic scenery and wildlife. There are very strong tidal currents running between the two harbours, which can churn up nasty tide rips in adverse conditions. The old slate quarry, which was previously protected by a rock wall, is now open to the sea through a couple of gaps in the rocks and provides shelter and private pontoons for the houses around it.

Access by road
Take the B844 from the Atlantic Bridge, signposted to the Cuan Ferry, then turn right at Balvicar, following the signposts to Ellenabeich.

Parking
There is a small car park on the pier and a larger one behind the visitor centre.

Water access
The channel between the two harbours can be approached from either side, with the pier remains providing a guide. Beacons mark rocks extending into the channel on the northwest side.

Facilities
Stores, Post Office, pub, restaurant and café cater for the needs of visitors. The village has its own brewery and an oyster restaurant as well as tourist attractions. There is also a visitor centre.

Further information
www.slateislands.org.uk
neil.brown@argyll-bute.gov.uk

Postcode
PA34 4RF

The remains of the pier used to ship out the slate. Easdale is in the background

The passenger ferry leaves Ellenabeich to cross to the island

Loch Feochan

History and comments

Loch Feochan, located between Easdale to the south and Oban to the north, has a challenging entrance via a channel that weaves between sandbanks. Because of this, many yachts would pass it by but the entrance channels are well marked with private buoys laid by the Ardoran Marine boatyard, based at Lerags on the north shore, and for peace and quiet it takes some beating. The boatyard is based at an old jetty, built out into the loch on a rocky spur by a local farmer many years ago. Today it is a well established yard with a pontoon and slipway that make it accessible at all states of tide. Its close proximity to Oban makes Ardoran Marine a useful facility, used mainly by local yachtsmen. The new boat shed and office built in 2011, principally using EU money, enable the yard to provide for most requirements. The boatyard offers a number of moorings for visiting yachts as well as winter storage facilities. Further along the north shore, to the west, is another pontoon jetty but this one is private and serves the small group of houses located at Ardentallan.

The private jetty and pontoon near the entrance to the loch

The main coast road runs close alongside the south side of the loch but there is surprisingly little development here and the loch remains a quiet and peaceful location, although traffic noise does carry from the busy main road during the summer months. The smart Knipoch Hotel is on the hill overlooking the south shore, whilst various logging operations are dotted along the north shore and an occasional ship comes in to load up with logs at the shore landing point established by the Forestry Commission. Historically, the loch was where the ancient kings of Scotland would pause on their journey out to Iona for burial. A white cottage overlooking the entrance provides a guide on the way in and was used for the filming of *Ring of Bright Water*, based on Gavin Maxwell's autobiographical tale of otters.

Access by road
Take the A816 heading south from Oban until the right-hand turn off to Lerags. Take this road and then follow a sign-posted turn to the left to Ardoran Marine.

Parking
Parking at the boatyard.

Water access
The white cottage provides a rough guide in. The narrow channel is marked by green and red buoys laid by the boatyard. Once clear of the entrance channel the loch is clear, except close to the shore.

Facilities
The boatyard caters for boating needs and the Foxholes Country Hotel is a couple of miles up the road.

More information
Ardoran Marine www.ardoran.co.uk

Postcode
PA34 4SE

Lerags is an idyllic place to moor but facilities are minimal

Lerags pier and pontoon created from an old farmer's jetty

Acknowledgements

My grateful thanks to the many helpful people I met along the way when researching this book. For me it was a labour of love and such a pleasure to meet the many fascinating people who live and work in this area.

My thanks, as always, also go to the people at Imray who do a great job of translating my words and pictures into lovely books.

Dag Pike, July 2015